FLY GUY PRESENTS: INSECTS

Tedd Arnold

Scholastic Inc.

For Dr. Margaret (Canopy Meg) Lowman,
biologist, explorer, educator, ecologist,
and fellow Elmiran!—T.A.

Photos ©: cover bee: Joel Sartore/National Geographic Creative; cover ant: DrPAS/Thinkstock; cover field and sky: elenavolkova/Thinkstock; cover caterpillar and ladybug on weed: Salvatore Volpes/Thinkstock; cover ant hill: PeterTG/Thinkstock; 4, 5 background: Marcin Okupniak/Dreamstime; 6 background, 7 background: Nils Weymann/Dreamstime; 6 map: Cartesia/Getty Images; 6 frame: Tadeusz Ibrom/Dreamstime; 7 center: CathyKeifer/iStockphoto; 7 top: Specker, Donald/Animals Animals; 7 bottom: Wild & Natural/Animals Animals; 8, 9 background: 1000 Words/Shutterstock, Inc.; 9 top left: Photo Researchers/Getty Images; 9 bottom left: francesco de marco/Shutterstock, Inc.; 9 top right: DEA PICTURE LIBRARY/Getty Images; 9 bottom right: johan63/iStockphoto; 10 top: fiulo/iStockphoto; 10 bottom: Wechsler, Doug/Animals Animals; 11 aphid: Bartomeu Borrell/Media Bakery; 11 eggs, 11 pupa: Perennou Nuridsany/Science Source; 11 larvae: smuay/Thinkstock; 11 adult: Nigel Cattlin/Science Source; 12 background, 13 background: chudoba/Shutterstock, Inc.; 12 inset: Cindy Creighton/Shutterstock, Inc.; 13 top: skynetphoto/Shutterstock, Inc.; 13 bottom: Beneda Miroslav/Shutterstock, Inc.; 14 background, 15: Chunli Li/Dreamstime; 14 top: Tokle/iStockphoto; 14 bottom: Wild & Natural/Animals Animals; 16 top left: Minden Pictures/Superstock, Inc.; 16 top right: Photo Quest Ltd/Science Photo Library/Corbis Images; 16 bottom left: hnijjaroo7/iStockphoto; 16 bottom right: Gewoldi/iStockphoto; 17 top right: Charles Krebs/Corbis Images; 17 bottom: Alex Wild/Corbis Images; 17 top left: Hans Lang/Corbis Images; 18 background, 19 background: Krasnevsky/iStockphoto; 18 center left: ntzolov/iStockphoto; 18 center right: tzooka/iStockphoto; 19 top: Pat Morris/Ardea; 19 bottom: Barnaby Chambers/Shutterstock, Inc.; 20 background bottom, 21 background bottom: Opas Chotiphantawanon/Shutterstock, Inc.; 20 background top: Johannesk/Dreamstime; 20 top: Paul Reeves Photography/Shutterstock, Inc.; 20 bottom: Katarina Christenson/Shutterstock, Inc.; 21 left: Clark, Jack/Animals Animals; 21 right: Specker, Donald/Animals Animals; 22: huePhotography/; 23 top: ivkuzmin/iStockphoto; 23 center: John Clegg/Ardea; 23 bottom: Piotr Naskrecki/Minden Pictures; 24 background, 25 background: mexrix/Shutterstock, Inc.; 24 bottom left: Rolf Nussbaumer/Corbis Images; 24 bottom right: Peter Macdiarmid/Reuters/Newscom; 24 top: Reyes Garcia III/USDA; 25 top: Jan Luit/Minden Pictures; 25 bottom: Ardea/Morris, Pat/Animals Animals; 26 background, 27 background: Johannes Kornelius/Shutterstock, Inc.; 26 inset: Tomatito/Shutterstock, Inc.; 27 inset: Pascal Goetgheluck/Ardea; 28 left: tunart/iStockphoto; 28 right: Minden Pictures/Superstock, Inc.; 29: Michele Menegon/Ardea; 30 background, 31 background: Pasticcio/iStockphoto; 30 right: Gavriel Jecan/Media Bakery; 30 left: Ratchapol Yindeesuk/Shutterstock, Inc.; 31 left: Chappell, Mark/Animals Animals; 31 right: Ardea/Sailer, Steffen & Alexandra/Animals Animals; 32: teo73/Thinkstock.

ISBN 978-0-545-75714-0

18 17 16   19 20/0

Printed in the U.S.A.   40

First printing, January 2015

A boy had a pet fly named Fly Guy.
Fly Guy could say the boy's name —

Buzz and Fly Guy were outside. Fly Guy wanted to look for insects. Buzz was a little worried.

"Some insects are scary," he said.

"I know, Fly Guy, you're an insect," said Buzz. "And you are not scary. I have nothing to be afraid of."

They set off to discover more.

There are more than one million different kinds of insects!

Insects live all over the world. They live on every continent — even Antarctica!

THE SEVEN CONTINENTS

NORTH AMERICA

EUROPE

ASIA

AFRICA

SOUTH AMERICA

AUSTRALIA

ANTARCTICA

Many people call insects "bugs." But not all insects are bugs. A bug is a kind of insect. Bugs have a mouth shaped like a straw. True bugs include milkweed bugs, boxelder bugs, and stinkbugs.

BOXELDER BUG

MILKWEED BUG

STINKBUG

Insects have been on Earth for hundreds of millions of years. They crawled and buzzed around even before the dinosaurs.

Long ago insects were much bigger than they are today.

A giant dragonfly's wings stretched over two feet long. That's the same as the wingspan of an arctic puffin.

GIANT DRAGONFLY

ARTHROPLEURA

ARCTIC PUFFIN

LION

Arthropleura (ar-throw-PLEW-rah) was like a giant centipede. It was six feet long. That's the average length of a lion!

All insects have a life cycle. A life cycle is made up of the changes that happen to the insect from the beginning of its life until it dies.

Most insects hatch from eggs. The insect grows into a larva (LAR-vuh). Fly larvae are called maggots.

MAGGOTZ

Larvae molt, or get rid of their old skin, to grow bigger.

molting cicada

Next, the insect becomes a pupa (PEW-puh). The pupa hides in a shell, or cocoon. There, it changes into an adult. This is called metamorphosis (meht-uh-MAWR-fuh-sihs).

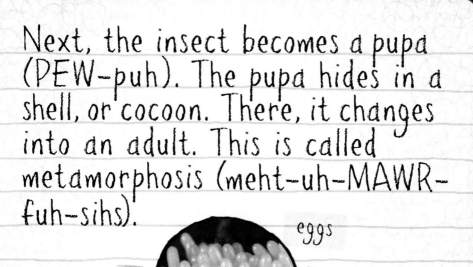

adult

eggs

METAMORPHOSIS

larvae

pupa

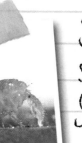

Some insects, such as aphids, give birth to live young.

aphid birth

A life span is the amount of time that a creature lives. Insects do not all have the same life span.

MAYFLY

Adult mayflies live for only one or two nights.

Some insects, such as a queen ant, can live for up to 30 years!

QUEEN ANT

ANT HILL

ANT EGGS

Insects have cool bodies! Mammals, like humans, have bones on the inside. But insects wear their hard parts on the outside. This is called an exoskeleton (ek-soh-SKEH-luh-tun).

• RHINO BEETLES •

An insect's body is made up of three parts: the head, the thorax, and the abdomen.

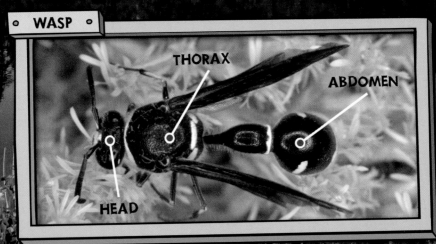

○ WASP ○

THORAX

ABDOMEN

HEAD

The head is where the eyes, mouthparts, and antennae (an-TEN-ay) are found. Antennae help insects taste, smell, touch, and even hear!

The thorax is the middle part of an insect. It holds the legs. All insects have six legs. The thorax also holds the wings, if the insect has them.

The abdomen holds the insect's stomach. If the insect has a stinger, it is found here.

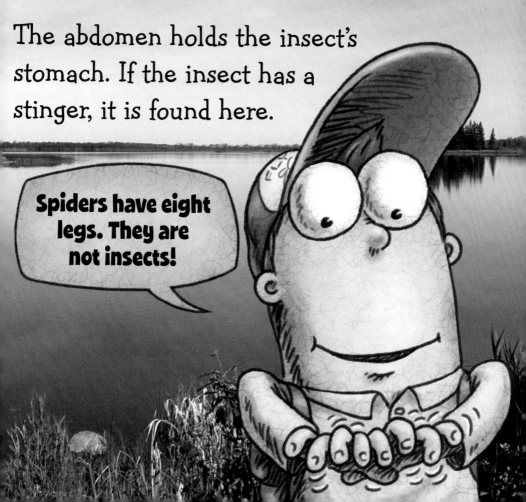

Spiders have eight legs. They are not insects!

Insects such as wasps, hornets, and some ants have stingers. Most of them use their stingers to protect themselves.

honeybee

Honeybees die after they use their stinger.

Some wasps use their stingers to catch food.

wasp

wasp stinger

hornet

STINGERZZZ!

bullet ant stinger

Usually, insects do not sting humans. But some insects will sting humans when they think they are in danger.

a red ant, ready to sting

For most people, insect stings are simply annoying and slightly painful or itchy. But some people are allergic to insect stings. They should seek medical care right away if stung.

Not all insects eat the same food.

Many insects munch on plants. Butterflies eat nectar (NEK-tur) from flowers.

○ SWALLOWTAIL BUTTERFLY ○

BLUE MORPHO BUTTERFLY

Other insects, such as mosquitoes, eat blood. To avoid bites, wear long sleeves and pants, and use insect repellent (rih-PEH-lunt) when outdoors.

Insects such as cockroaches and ants eat almost anything — even crumbs on the floor.

COCKROACHES

COCKROACH

Fly Guy, that's gross!

MUNCH CRUNCH

Insects also have different ways of eating. Some insects, like grasshoppers and caterpillars, chew their food. Other insects suck it up using a special body part called a proboscis (pro-BAHS-siss).

GRASSHOPPER

CATERPILLAR

Mosquitoes suck food up like they are drinking through a straw. The straw is the proboscis.

Some insects seem to have superpowers.

There are insects that can glow! This is called bioluminescence (by-oh-loo-mih-NEH-suhns).

fireflies

Fireflies, also called lightning bugs, are not really flies or bugs. They are beetles! They have special chemicals in their abdomens. When the chemicals meet oxygen (AHKS-ih-jen), the fireflies' abdomens light up.

Fireflies use their lights to help find other fireflies. They also light up to warn animals not to eat them—the glowing chemicals taste bad!

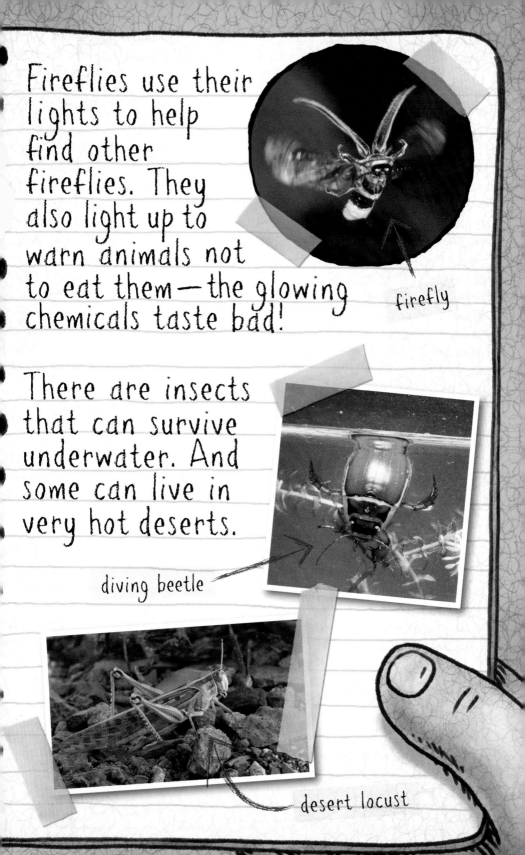

firefly

There are insects that can survive underwater. And some can live in very hot deserts.

diving beetle

desert locust

The world is full of amazing insects.

FAIRYFLY

Fairyflies are the smallest insects on Earth. These wasps can only be seen under a microscope!

The longest insect is Chan's megastick. It is 22 inches long!

Harvester ants are the most poisonous insects on the planet.

HARVESTER ANT

CHAN'S MEGASTICK

In the air, the Southern giant darner dragonfly is the speediest insect. It can fly as fast as a car going 35 miles per hour!

○ DARNER DRAGONFLY ○

On land, the speed record goes to the cockroach. Cockroaches can run at about three and a half miles per hour.

○ COCKROACH ○

Cockroaches are tough. They can live for days without a head!

Flies are awesome insects!

There are 120,000 species (SPEE-sheez), or types, of flies. All flies are in the order Diptera. And a person who studies or collects flies is called a dipterist.

Flies' eyes are special — they have compound eyes. Compound eyes are not good at seeing far away. But they are great at detecting movement.

FLYZZZ!

COMPOUND EYES HAVE MANY DIFFERENT LENSES TO SEE OUT OF. EACH EYE CAN HAVE UP TO 30,000 DIFFERENT LENSES.

• FLY EYES •

• WHAT FLY EYES SEE •

If something gets close, a fly can plan an escape route in less than one second!

Most flies don't bite animals. But some flies, like deerflies and horseflies, do. They drink blood.

Flies sleep a lot! They sleep between nine and 15 hours each night.

DEERFLY

A fly's wings beat 200 times per second.

Scientists who study insects
are called entomologists
(en-tuh-MAHL-uh-jists).

entomologists at work

Entomologists sometimes go
on expeditions (ex-puh-
DIH-shunz), or special trips
to look for insects. They
study insects where they live.
And they live everywhere!

Insects live in treetops, in hot deserts, underground, on animals, and even in frozen Antarctica.

IN JARZ TOO!

Millions of insects live in tropical rain forests. Most of them live in the canopy layer, or the tops of trees. As many as 1,000 different types of insects have been found in just <u>one</u> tree in a rain forest canopy!

canopy layer

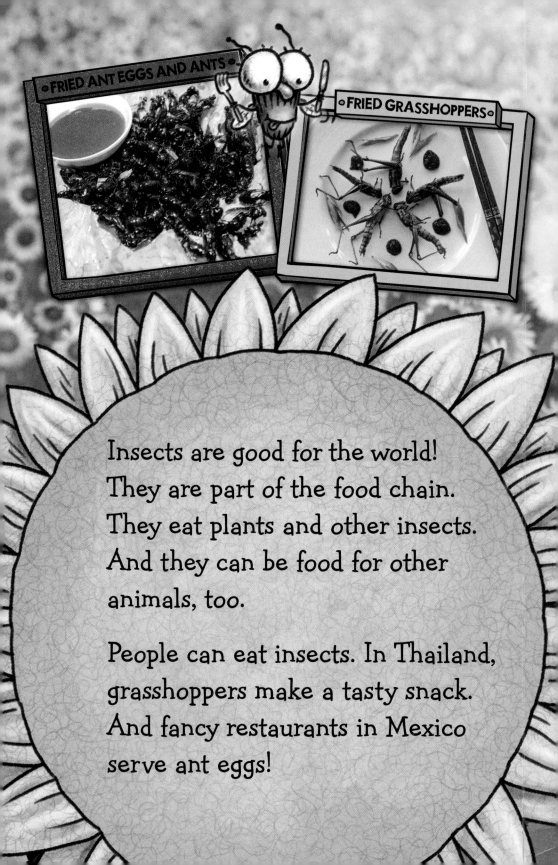

•FRIED ANT EGGS AND ANTS•

•FRIED GRASSHOPPERS•

Insects are good for the world!
They are part of the food chain.
They eat plants and other insects.
And they can be food for other
animals, too.

People can eat insects. In Thailand,
grasshoppers make a tasty snack.
And fancy restaurants in Mexico
serve ant eggs!

Insects are important to us! Plants would not be able to grow without them.

When insects, such as bees and butterflies, land on flowers, they pollinate (PAH-lih-nayt) them. Only then can fruits and vegetables grow.

BEES ON HONEYCOMB

BEE POLLINATING A CHERRY TREE

Bees also make honey. Yum!

"Insects are great!" said Buzz. "I didn't know they were *so* amazing."

Now Buzz knew for sure that Fly Guy was the coolest pet on the planet!

Buzz and Fly Guy couldn't wait for their next adventure.